BLACKBOARD, BLACKBOARD ON THE WALL, WHO IS THE FAIREST ONE OF ALL?

DEDICATED TO THOSE TEACHERS
WHO SEE CHILDREN
AS MORE THAN A TICKET
TO A SUMMER VACATION.

Albert Cullum

BLACKBOARD, BLACKBOARD ON THE WALL, WHO IS THE FAIREST ONE OF ALL?

A Harlin Quist Book

BY ALBERT CULLUM

Published by Harlin Quist, Inc.
Library of Congress Catalog Card: 78-70569
ISBN: 0-8252-0728-2
Text and illustrations copyright © 1978
by Harlin Quist. All rights reserved.
First printing. Printed in the U.S.A.

PUBLISHER'S NOTE:
What is a Teacher?
Babysitter? Inspiration?
Disciplinarian? Advisor? Substitute parent?...
or the image we keep, no matter how long ago
we left school behind: Teacher at the big desk,
knowing everything, seeing everything, heavy with power.
Here in the pages of this book are the Teachers.
People, like all of us, trying, like all of us, to cope.
With children, with lessons, with administrators,
with new methods for old teachers
and old prejudices for new ones.
With parents—oh! those parents!
Here are Teachers loving "their" children—
except sometimes, when things get out of hand
and they lose sight of love. Here are Teachers
trying to share the excitement of learning
with the young lives that drew them into teaching—
all the while trying to hang on to lives of their own.
Be sure the children see
BLACKBOARD, BLACKBOARD ON THE WALL,
WHO IS THE FAIREST ONE OF ALL?
It's for them, so they can find out who Teacher is.
Their Teacher is in these pages.
Everyone's Teacher is.

New faces every September ...
Maybe this year, I'll find a poet!
A scientist!
A dancer!
A writer!
Maybe this year ...

I say it to them every day:
"Don't be afraid, boys and girls.
It's o.k. to make a mistake.
It's even o.k. to cry.
Be brave. Take chances."
I wish I dared tell them
I'm still afraid of the dark.

"Be proud, children. Like yourselves.
You don't have to be smart.
You don't have to wear nice clothes.
Just like yourselves.
Not next year — now!"

The children are o.k. —
even the ones who are fresh.
I can cope with them.
After all, they're children.
But oh! those parents! . . .
Yes, yes, I know:
no parents, no kids, no job.

I'm dedicated to my work, to my students.
My lesson plans are always up to date.
My bulletin boards are colorful.
My class is my life.
I'm dedicated — until the last bell rings.
I've got to have that other time to be me.

How do I say,
"Your son is not stupid,
but he's not very bright either."
How do I tell the parents
that he's just an average kid —
like them!

That old bat next door thinks she knows it all!
Her quiet room . . . that perfect penmanship.
And she never raises her voice.
Those kids are so scared they don't dare breathe!

aBCr

aBCr

aBCr

aBCr

Neil Waldman

My kindergarten children are so sweet,
so cute I could eat them up!
Some day I hope to have a baby of my own —
but in the meantime,
I'm glad I'm a kindergarten teacher.

Those older kids make me nervous:
they're always challenging me.
But the little ones trust me completely:
they believe everything I say . . .
But boy! I'm glad I've got those teachers' guides!

Spelling's done.
Arithmetic — sort of.
We covered Asia.
And sandwiched in creative writing.
Thank god it's Friday!
The horror show is over!

This class is worse than last year's!
That first year teacher prepared them for nothing!
They need drill, drill, and more drill!
I'll drill them!
— right through the wall!

Many Marias,
a Jorge, a Ramon, an Eduardo,
Jesus (two of them),
Cammillo and his sister Consuelo,
Diego, Pedro, Luisa . . .
What can I, Nancy Smith from Maple Road, teach them?
What can they learn from me?

Wish I could be the phys ed teacher
just for a day or two.
How happy the kids are on the playground,
in the gym.
And the phys ed teacher
is always the favorite!

They send those kids to me day in and day out —
reading problems of all kinds.
Yes, their reading improves.
But they need more, so much more.
And I'm no miracle worker.

It's P.T.A. night.
I'll have to smile a lot
and answer ten thousand questions.
Questions all day from the children.
Questions again at night.
What makes them think I know all the answers?
I have some questions too...

I don't know why I don't like that kid —
but I don't.
I like all the others,
even the noisy ones.
There's just something about that kid
that makes me hope she'll make another mistake.

Mary has two fathers,
David drinks coke for breakfast,
Helen has bruises on her arms . . .
Sometimes I feel I'm all they've got.
I have to be what they need!
But it's getting harder and harder to smile.

"Accountability?"
I'll give that principal "accountability"
until he chokes on it!
Those flow charts are going to flow
even if it kills these kids!

Who needs this crap?
Who needs these fourth grade brats
and their pushy parents
and that stupid curriculum director?
I don't need this rat race!
My husband makes good money!
Someday I'll quit!
Someday . . .

Let's paint a mural!
Let's put on a play!
Dream with me, boys and girls!
Dream big — and someday you may do big!

Oh, oh!
Here comes a school board member!
And this is "Balanced Diet Week!"
I can't help it, I really can't!
Spring vacation is almost over,
and I need some cheering up.
Teachers are human too!

That child seems to do everything wrong.
He's messy. He daydreams. He passes notes.
I don't know why I'm so patient with him, but I am.
Maybe it's the way he grins at me
just after he's done something devilish.
That smile makes up for a lot!

Do you love your teacher, children?
Do you think I'm important?
Do you think I'm the best?
Tell me, boys and girls, tell me:
am I the fairest one of all? . . .

Oh, no! Tomorrow's Monday!
I'll call in sick!
Let the substitute go bananas!
56 more days to go!
56 more days of screaming!
I can't call in sick 56 times!

"One more crack from that kid and she's going out the window!"
"That substitute set me back a week!"
"What do you mean I don't have a free period this afternoon?"
"Don't they ever bathe!?"
"Who promoted that dummy?!"
"Damn it! There's the bell!"

Some of them will be in trouble
by the time they get to high school.
I can always tell which ones:
when I talk to them, they smirk
and look right through me.
How can I wake them up?
Get through to them? Save them?
Even one.

It's June, and it's over.
The quizzes, the tests —
they passed them all.
But I never found time to get to know them . . .

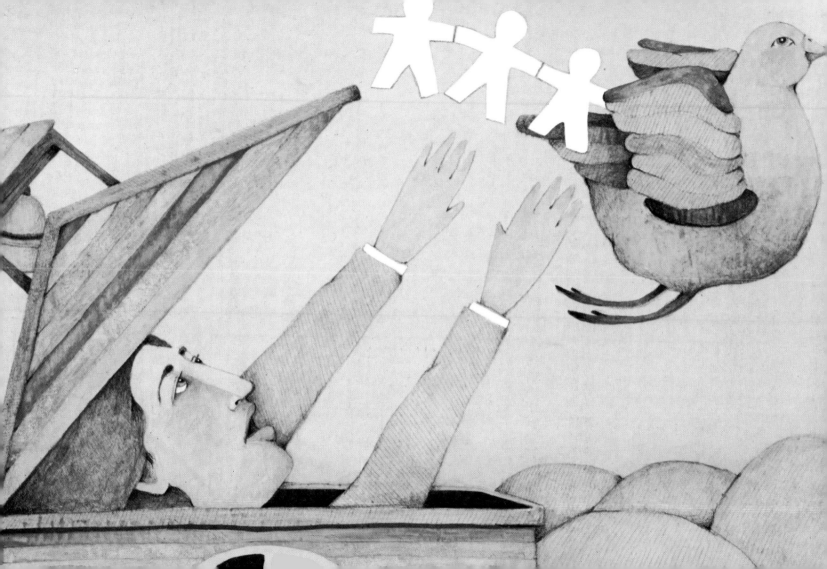

I wake up at night dreaming of hands.
I see them everywhere I go.
Hands reaching out for help, for attention,
for contact, for more than I know how to give.
Hands down, children! Hands down!

The illustrators:
Jacques Rozier and Monique Gaudriault/8
Jözef Sumichrast/11
Dagmar Frinta/13
Slug Signorino/15
Gilles Bachelet/17
Joel Naprstek/19
Neil Waldman/21
Cathy Deeter/23
Bernard Bonhomme/25
Jöel Le Berre/27
Slug Signorino/29
Joel Naprstek/31
Elwood Smith/33
Bernard Bonhomme/35
Slug Signorino/37
Cathy Deeter/39
Jacques Rozier and Monique Guadriault/41
Jözef Sumichrast/43
Cathy Deeter/45
France de Ranchin/47
Elwood Smith/49
Jöel Le Berre/51
Joel Naprstek/53
Victoria Chess/55
Slug Signorino/57
Joel Naprstek/59
Dagmar Frinta/61
Philippe Corre/63
Tina Mercie/cover
and title page illustrations